Spot the Difference

# Ears

Daniel Nunn

**www.heinemann.co.uk/library**
Visit our website to find out more information about **Heinemann Library** books.

To order:
☎ Phone 44 (0) 1865 888066
▤ Send a fax to 44 (0) 1865 314091
▢ Visit the Heinemann Bookshop at www.heinemann.co.uk/library to browse our catalogue and order online.

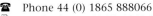

First published in Great Britain by Heinemann Library, Halley Court, Jordan Hill, Oxford OX2 8EJ, part of Harcourt Education. Heinemann is a registered trademark of Harcourt Education Ltd.

Editorial: Tracey Crawford, Cassie Mayer, Dan Nunn, and Sarah Chappelow
Design: Jo Hinton-Malivoire
Picture Research: Erica Newbery
Production: Duncan Gilbert

Originated by RMW
Printed and bound in China by South China Printing Company

10 digit ISBN 0 431 18237 X
13 digit ISBN 978 0 431 18237 7

11 10 09 08 07
10 9 8 7 6 5 4 3 2 1

**British Library Cataloguing in Publication Data**
Nunn, Daniel
Ears. - (Spot the difference)
1.Ear - Juvenile literature 2.Hearing - Juvenile literature
I.Title
573.8'9
A full catalogue record for this book is available from the British Library.

**Acknowledgements**
The publishers would like to thank the following for permission to reproduce photographs: Ardea pp. **10** (John Daniels), **11** (Ken Lucas), **12** (Bob Gibbons), **14** (blickwinkel), **15** (Adams Picture Library), **20** (bilderlounge); FLPA p. **18** (Minden Pictures/ZSSD); Getty Images pp. **4** (Stone/Time Flachs), **21** (GettyImages/Photodisc Red/PNC); Nature Picture Library pp. **5** (T.J. Rich), **6** (Mike Wilkes), **7** (Lynn M. Stone), **8** (Anup Shah), **9** (Meul/ARCO), **13** (David Pike), **16** (David Kjaer), **17** (Bruce Davidson), **19** (Dagmar G. Wolf).

Cover photograph of a lynx reproduced with permission of Nature Picture Library/Graham Hatherley.

Every effort has been made to contact copyright holders of any material reproduced in this book. Any omissions will be rectified in subsequent printings if notice is given to the publishers.

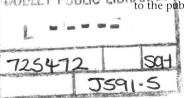

# Contents

# What are ears?

ear

Why do animals have ears?

Animals use their ears to hear.

# Where are animals' ears?

Most animals have ears on
their head.

This is a donkey.
It has ears on top
of its head.

This is a chimpanzee.
It has ears on the sides of its head.

ear

This is a cricket.
It has ears on its legs.
Can you spot the difference?

# Different ears

Ears come in many shapes and sizes.

This is a bat-eared fox.
It has big ears.

This is a sea lion.
It has small ears.

This is a wolf.
It has pointy ears.

This is a koala.
It has round ears.

This is a lop-eared rabbit.
It has floppy ears.
Can you spot the difference?

# Amazing ears

This is an owl.
It can hear from high up in the sky.

This is an elephant.
It flaps its ears to keep cool.

This is a hippo.
It closes its ears to keep water out.

This is a bat.
It uses its ears to find its way.

# Your ears

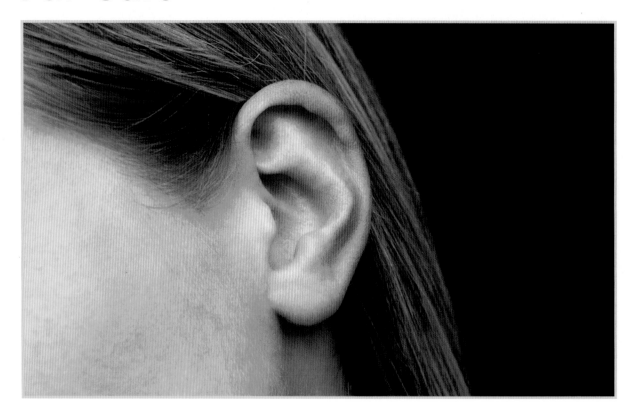

People have ears, too. Like animals, people use their ears to hear.

What can these children hear?

# Can you remember?

Which of these animals flaps its ears to keep cool?

# Picture glossary

 **floppy** soft, not firm

 **hear** listen to sounds using your ears

 **pointy** sharp at one end

 **round** shaped like a circle

# Index

**Notes to parents and teachers**

**Before reading**

Talk about how we use our ears to hear. Tell the children to put their hands over their ears and say "I use my ears to hear". Can they hear their own voice in their heads?

**After reading**

Play "Guess the sound": Show the children a glass, a wooden spoon, a fork and plate. Tap each object in turn with a pencil and tell the children to listen carefully to each sound. Then tell the children to turn away so they can't see the objects. Tap an object with the pencil and ask a child to say which object is being tapped.

Play the "Whispering game": Whisper a sentence to one child and tell them to pass on the sentence by whispering it to the next child. Ask the last child in the line what they heard. How does it compare with the original sentence?

# Titles in the *Spot the Difference* series include:

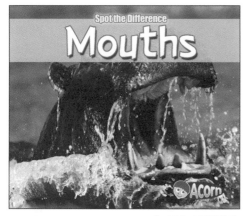

Hardback            0 431 18239 6

Hardback            0 431 18238 8

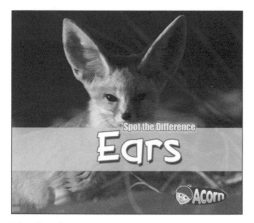

Hardback            0 431 18237 X

Hardback            0 431 18236 1

Find out about other titles from Heinemann Library on our website www.heinemann.co.uk/library